THE 10

Deadliest Plants

Angie Littlefield • Jennifer Littlefield

Series Editor
Jeffrey D. Wilhelm

Much thought, debate, and research went into choosing and ranking the 10 items in each book in this series. We realize that everyone has his or her own opinion of what is most significant, revolutionary, amazing, deadly, and so on. As you read, you may agree with our choices, or you may be surprised — and that's the way it should be!

Franklin Watts®

an imprint of

◢SCHOLASTIC

www.scholastic.com/librarypublishing

A Rubicon book published in association with Scholastic Inc.

Ru'bicon © 2008 Rubicon Publishing Inc.
www.rubiconpublishing.com

Associate Publishers: Kim Koh, Miriam Bardswich
Project Editor: Amy Land
Editor: Christine Boocock
Creative Director: Jennifer Drew
Project Manager/Designer: Jeanette MacLean
Graphic Designer: Rebecca Buchanan

The publisher gratefully acknowledges the following for permission to reprint copyrighted material in this book.

Every reasonable effort has been made to trace the owners of copyrighted material and to make due acknowledgment. Any errors or omissions drawn to our attention will be gladly rectified in future editions.

"Mr. Stinky Blooms" (excerpt). From *As it Happens, Voice of the World*, CBC Radio One.

"Alien Plant Invasion" (excerpt from "Swallowwort") by Gerry Rising in *Buffalo Sunday News*, June 26, 2005. Permission courtesy of Gerry Rising.

"Exoskeletons and Other Remains" by Dr. Barry Rice, The International Carnivorous Plant Society. Permission courtesy of Dr. Barry Rice.

"Poison Hemlock 101" from e-mail sent by Dr. Steven Dewey, April 2, 2007. Permission courtesy of Dr. Steven Dewey.

Cover: Venus flytrap catches fly–©DAVID M. DENNIS/Animals Animals–Earth Scenes–All rights reserved

Library and Archives Canada Cataloguing in Publication

Littlefield, Angie
    The 10 deadliest plants / Angie Littlefield and Jennifer Littlefield.

Includes index.
ISBN 978-1-55448-511-6

    1. Readers (Elementary). 2. Readers—Plants. I. Littlefield, Jennifer II. Title. III. Title: Ten deadliest plants.

PE1117.L6733 2007a   428.6   C2007-906707-7

1 2 3 4 5 6 7 8 9 10   10   17 16 15 14 13 12 11 10 09 08

Printed in Singapore

Contents

6

22

38

VICIOUS

When you step out for a hike or go camping in the woods, you wear the right shoes, take lots of supplies, and prepare for whatever mother nature might throw at you. But what if you should get lost? What if those supplies ran out and you were starving? Would you be tempted to nibble a little greenery or some shiny berries? If you said yes, this book's for you!

Plants are vital to our survival, but not all of them are good for you. Some plants are poisonous. Others can strangle, smother, and suck the life out of insects or other plants. There are dangers lurking out there in the green world!

In this book, we present what we think are the 10 deadliest plants. Some of these plants make people sick; others can actually kill. Some kill off their victims, whether insects, animals, or humans, very quickly. Others work at a slower pace. Some plants are less dangerous because they grow in remote places people wouldn't likely go to; others grow in very populated areas and are a real danger. The most dangerous plants are those that look like common plants and can be easily mistaken for something harmless.

You'll be shocked when you discover the truth behind the innocent-looking greenery in your home, garden, and parks.

Get informed — recognizing the 10 deadliest plants could save your life!

VEGETATION

WHICH DO YOU THINK IS THE DEADLIEST PLANT?

Nicknamed "Ted the Titan" by its keepers at the University of California, this plant grew to be about six feet tall. This photograph shows it at its maximum stinkiness.

SCIENTIFIC NAME: *Amorphophallus titanum* (uh-mawr-fuh-fah-lus tie-tan-um)

NITTY-GRITTY: No wonder it's called a "titan" — this plant has a giant blossom that can grow to almost 10 ft. tall. The other half of this plant's name, arum, comes from its botanical family.

DEADLY DETAILS: Its deadly aroma can be detected almost one mile away.

It may have a spectacular blossom, but the titan arum is not the kind of plant you'd want in your house. Instead of the usual fragrant scent of flowers, a flowering titan arum gives off a smell like that of rotting flesh! And the stink is so powerful it can be smelled from almost a mile away!

The titan arum's deadly stink is a great tool for pollination. Some bugs like to lay their eggs on rotting flesh. Because the titan arum smells like decaying flesh, insects flock to it. In the process, they spread the titan arum pollen from one flower to another. So, even though it makes people want to run the other way, the titan arum's smell actually ensures its survival.

The plant's toxic properties cause irritation if ingested. But as the world's biggest stinker, the titan arum still has a huge fan club. People line up to see this rare and endangered flower. Believe it or not, many also want to experience its killer smell for themselves!

TITAN ARUM

HOME GROUND

This rare plant is native to the hot and humid tropical rain forests of Sumatra, Indonesia. Titan arums grow from a large tuber, or underground stem. A single one of these can weigh up to 220 pounds! An Italian botanist named Odoardo Beccari first discovered the titan arum in 1878 in Sumatra. He took some seeds back to Italy. Small plants grown from the seeds were eventually taken to England's Royal Botanical Gardens.

IF LOOKS COULD KILL ...

The titan arum only flowers once every few years, but it's worth the wait! The giant flower can grow to over nine feet tall — almost the height of a basketball hoop! It is pale green on the outside and burgundy inside. This deep red color contributes to the illusion that it is a piece of rotting meat. The central part of the flower is pale yellow and stands upright. Titan arums only bloom for four or five days, which is a good thing, since this is when their stench is strongest!

Quick Fact

The titan arum is very hard to cultivate. The first cultivated bloom was in England's Royal Botanical Gardens in 1889. This was when one of Odoardo Beccari's small plants first bloomed! The event generated so much excitement that police were called in for crowd control.

cultivate: *grow; nurture*

? If the titan arum is such a hard plant to cultivate, why did people try so hard to do it?

The Expert Says...

" The odor comes out in waves. ... It's about every 10 or 15 minutes; it all of a sudden gets piercingly strong. ... Oh, it makes your eyes water, it's something else. "

— Craig Allen, former conservation manager, Fairchild Tropical Botanic Garden

KISS OF DEATH

The toxic, needle-shaped calcium oxalate crystals in titan arums can irritate skin. If eaten, they lodge in the soft tissue of the mouth and throat and cause swelling, difficulty breathing, and sometimes suffocation.

The titan arum has suffered from a case of mistaken identity for years. Because of its smell of rotting corpses, people in Indonesia considered it deadly. They thought the plant was carnivorous, or meat eating, because of the smell. They called the flower *bunga bangka*, which means "corpse flower." They would destroy the flowers to avoid being eaten by them!

calcium oxalate: *chemical compound of calcium and an acid*

The pungent smelling titan arum is one of the world's largest flowers.

Mr. Stinky Blooms

✳ From *As It Happens* CBC Radio One

People everywhere get excited when one of these rare flowers blooms! In this interview, Canadian Broadcasting Corporation (CBC) radio host Mary Lou Finlay talks to conservation manager Craig Allen of the Fairchild Tropical Garden in Miami.

✳   ✳   ✳

Mary Lou Finlay: Mr. Allen, just how stinky is Mr. Stinky?

CA: Well, right at the moment he doesn't smell much at all. But … two nights ago I probably would've been so ill I would've had a hard time telling you.

MF: Was that the height of his stinkiness?

CA: Yeah … it smelled like a truckload of fish that had laid out in the sun for about five days … [It] was powerful. In its native habitat they claim that it smells like a rotted elephant corpse. … [The odor] only lasts about 10 hours. And, although it's really bad for that 10 hours that's also the most interesting time to be around it.

MF: Why?

CA: Because it's opening, at that period. To watch this flower … that's like almost seven foot tall, opening up over a five-hour period, is pretty intriguing. …

MF: Well, how close can you get to it? When it's in full stench?

CA: Well, I get up really close … [At] one point I thought I was going to have to put on a gas mask. But, it's hard to take pictures when you have a mask on. … And, … the coroner's office, the time we had one bloom in '98, they brought me a bottle of wintergreen oil. And they use it to apply to their upper lip. And while you still smell the smell, the nausea goes away. … [It's] a lot more bearable. Still, it could barely overcome the power this thing had over us.

Quick Fact

Titan arums can generate their own heat. Revving up their built-in furnaces helps them spread their scent. This lures more insects toward them and increases chances of pollination.

Take Note

A plant that tries to pass itself off as rotting flesh deserves the #10 spot on our list of deadly plants. Its toxic properties add to its deadly profile, even if few people would want a taste of this super stinker!
• Would you want to get a firsthand look at a titan arum? Explain why or why not.

Strangler figs are considered a "keystone" species. This is because of their important place in their ecosystem. Despite the danger they pose to other trees, many animals rely on the fruit of the strangler for survival.

FIG

SCIENTIFIC NAME: *Ficus aurea* (fie-cuss ar-ee-uh)

NITTY-GRITTY: The strangler fig can grow up to 150 ft. tall. It is the common name for several species of fig tree.

DEADLY DETAILS: Stranglers attach themselves to "host plants." They feed off their hosts and then squeeze them to death!

Imagine an uninvited guest dropping by your home — and then eating up all your food and eventually squeezing the life out of you. That's exactly what the strangler fig does!

It's safe to say that the strangler fig wouldn't win any good neighbor awards from other trees in the rain forest! The struggle for territory starts when sticky fig seeds land on a tree — via animal droppings. The seeds produce shoots that reach down to the ground. Once on the ground, they grow roots — which compete with the host tree's roots for water and nutrients. Some of the shoots turn into hard vines. These vines cling tightly on the host tree, growing around and around it. In the end, the strangler fig sucks the life right out of its unlucky host!

While it's an enemy to trees, this deadly strangler is popular with many kinds of animals. That's because strangler figs grow small, dark purple fruit that birds, monkeys, and bats feed on.

STRANGLER FIG

Strangler fig berries and a fruit dove

HOME GROUND

Strangler figs thrive in steamy climates and areas of heavy rainfall. They are found in tropical locales all over the world. Specifically, stranglers can be found in the hot jungles of the Caribbean, South and Central America, and South Asia.

? There are many different types of parasitic plants. Do some research and find out which ones are dangerous to humans, animals, and other vegetation.

IF LOOKS COULD KILL ...

Even in the dense rain forest, stranglers are easy to spot. Stranglers have wide, oval-shaped leaves that measure between two to four inches in length. The strangler's vines grab hold of the host like the tentacles of an octopus. It can take years for a strangler fig to choke the life out of a host tree. When the host tree dies and rots away, the hollow strangler is left behind — an eerie sight to behold.

KISS OF DEATH

The strangler fig is a parasite. This means that it lives off something else. It starts as a humble seed but the strangler follows a process of total domination! Since the strangler starts life at the top of the forest canopy, its leaves get all the sunlight. The thick leaves of the strangler fig shade the host and block it from receiving essential sunshine.

As they grow, stranglers crush whatever they are growing on and have even been blamed for destroying buildings and ancient ruins!

Tha Prohm, Angkor Wat, Cambodia

The Expert Says ...

"In spite of their sinister common name, strangler figs are important components of forest ecosystems ... [They] produce three or more crops of fruit a year, providing food ... when other sources are in short supply.

— Gene McAvoy, University of Florida

components: *parts*

Protective Poisons

Deadly plants leave animal, insect, plant, and even human corpses in their wake. Find out more them in this article.

As with other forms of life — from animals to bacteria — plants have only two objectives: to survive and to reproduce. The poisonous substances in killer plants protect them from being plucked, harvested, or eaten. These substances discourage animals from munching on poisonous plants. They make insects look for pollen elsewhere. The fact that these substances can harm or kill insects, animals, or people, is an unfortunate side effect.

Killer plants use their flowers, smells, vines, and other adaptations to reproduce more effectively. Plants need pollinators, sunlight, and space to help them reproduce. The poisonous substances found in many plants also help with reproduction. A plant that is safe from predators can reproduce more effectively.

? Plants really only have two goals in life: to survive and to create more plants! The strangler fig distributes its seeds in the fruit that is eaten by birds and animals. How else do plants spread their seeds?

Quick Fact

Animals love figs because they are sweet and tasty. Figs are also high in fiber. Thanks to this dietary nutrient, animals produce more droppings. More droppings mean more strangler seeds will be spread!

Take Note

The strangler fig may not be a host tree's best friend, but it's hardly a threat to humanity. Only trees need fear the grip of a strangler fig, so this tree ranks #9.
• The strangler fig is deadlier than the titan arum. Which one do you think is more beneficial to its ecosystem and why?

Each swallowwort seed is able to produce two to four baby plants.

SCIENTIFIC NAME: *Cynanchum nigrum* (sahy-nan-chum ny-grum) (black swallowwort); *cynanchum rossicum* (sahy-nan-chum ros-ih-kum) (pale swallowwort)

NITTY-GRITTY: Swallowwort can grow to be over 6 ft. tall and can cover large areas of space. This vine is almost impossible to get rid of. Its seeds are spread by the wind and once they land, they stick!

DEADLY DETAILS: Swallowwort literally swallows up the space in which it grows and anything that happens to get in its way! It's a natural smotherer.

This plant has a ruthless ability to kill vegetation and insects. It also has an awesome ability to spread through its environment, smothering everything along the way. The plant's natural poisons make it unappealing to wildlife so animals won't eat it. In North America, swallowwort has few natural enemies, making it even harder to control.

An invasive, uncontrollable killer that destroys all foliage in its path, swallowwort makes a perfect fit for the #8 spot on our list.

_____

invasive: *having a tendency to spread and destroy*
foliage: *plant or tree leaves*

? What is the difference between vines that creep along the ground and those that climb into the air? Do some research on these varieties of vines and name some common types of each.

SWALLOWWORT

HOME GROUND

Swallowwort is not only highly invasive, but it can thrive in shade, sun, and all soil conditions. It is originally from parts of Europe, like Italy, France, Portugal, Spain, and southern Russia, where native insects and diseases naturally control its spread. In North America, though, the swallowwort has no natural enemy.

> Swallowwort has spread so rampantly because it has no natural enemies in North America. How might scientists and gardeners learn how to stop the spread of this plant?

IF LOOKS COULD KILL ...

There are two main varieties of this vine — pale and black swallowwort. The leaves of both varieties are heart-shaped, dark green, and smooth. The flowers appear in late May to early June. They are star-shaped with five petals. The flowers of the pale swallowwort are pinkish to beige. Black swallowwort has dark maroon flowers. Each pod produces many silky-haired seeds that float easily in the wind. No wonder it spreads so fast!

Quick Fact

Swallowwort is especially dangerous to monarch butterflies. They mistake swallowwort for milkweed plants and lay their eggs in the wrong place. Caterpillars that hatch on swallowwort don't survive. This has badly affected monarch populations.

KISS OF DEATH

Swallowwort spreads in the same way as dandelions. All those fluffy seeds blow in the wind and are hard to stop. Once they land, the seeds immediately start to grow. They develop into a tangled mess of vines, smothering existing plants and stealing sunlight and nutrients. Underground, swallowwort roots grow into the soil. Each root has a bud that will immediately grow if the plant is cut or damaged. The moral of the story? If you see this plant in your garden, remove it immediately, roots and all!

Swallowwort seeds are attached to fluffs that blow in the wind. This allows them to be carried great distances.

The Expert Says...

> Despite botanists' warnings ... this plant has attracted little attention until recently, as managers and conservationists have become increasingly alarmed by its rapid spread.

— Naomi Cappuccino, Associate Professor of Biology, Carleton University, Ottawa, Ontario

ALIEN PLANT INVASION

Pale swallowwort flowers are light pink in color.

Swallowwort grows fast and climbs all over other vegetation, smothering it.

A newspaper article from *Buffalo Sunday News,* June 26, 2005
By Gerry Rising

Julie West lives in Henderson, New York, ... "To me," she says, "it's like my land has cancer and I feel an overwhelming sense of helplessness as I watch swallowwort spread. [At first] it's very deceiving. It's just a plant here, a plant there, no big deal." But then, she says, over very few years it multiplies "until it is so thick it completely smothers everything. It twines together so you can hardly walk through it. Nothing else grows, not even grass. ... It can climb eight to 10 feet high. It will smother and kill juniper, honeysuckle, and small trees."

Andrew Fowler, who manages a Christmas tree farm and nursery southeast of Rochester, New York, first came across swallowwort about seven years ago. ... "It was when I was mowing a wooded slope one fall that I realized that this was no ordinary weed. The entire trail and surrounding woods was a mass of swallowwort six or seven feet tall, clambering over the undergrowth and up the trees."... Soon it began to take over his Christmas tree plantation, growing, he says, "in the grassy aisles between the trees, crowding out everything else. I began efforts at controlling it by spraying herbicides, but nothing seemed to kill it ... I believe that the application of herbicides actually gave it a competitive edge by killing off its competition ... it has spread to every corner of our farm."

Quick Fact

For swallowwort seeds and roots to be destroyed, they have to be put into paper bags, dried out, and then burned. Another method is to boil the seeds and roots for about 10 minutes before disposal.

Take Note

Swallowwort's aggressive attitude and amazing fertility make it a huge threat to native vegetation. Home gardeners and farmers alike fear this plant. It attacks budding crops and young trees, so it is dangerous to ecosystems and agriculture. Swallowwort doesn't kill animals or humans though, so it ranks #8 on our list.

• Since the strangler fig is a natural predator, it has an important place in its native ecosystem. Swallowwort, however, invades places where it doesn't naturally grow. Which one do you think is more dangerous to its environment? Explain your answer.

These traps may be scary-looking, but they're vulnerable too. Each trap can only catch and digest insects a few times during its lifetime. So this plant has to be picky about what it eats!

AP

SCIENTIFIC NAME: *Dionaea muscipula* (dy-oh-nee-uh mus-kip-you-luh)

NITTY-GRITTY: Venus flytraps are generally no bigger than 4 in. in diameter. Each trap measures between 1 and 3 in. long. A single plant can have up to 20 traps.

DEADLY DETAILS: Venus flytraps have a taste for flesh!

A carnivorous plant may sound like something out of a horror movie. But the Venus flytrap is a real-life meat-eater! Apart from their meat-munching ways, though, these plants also have a reputation for speed. They are one of the fastest movers in the plant world when they're looking for a meal! The Venus flytrap sits quietly for hours waiting for its prey. The moment an unsuspecting visitor arrives, the Venus flytrap jumps into action. As soon as an insect touches the sensitive cilia, or hairs, located on the inside of a Venus flytrap's leaves, it snaps shut. And there's no chance of escape — the Venus flytrap closes faster than you can blink. It takes just one-tenth of a second to trap its guest! And what happens to the bug stuck inside? Guess who's invited to dinner?

? There are many plants in the world that eat insects and other small animals. Find out about other carnivorous plants.

VENUS FLYTRAP

HOME GROUND

Venus flytraps are native to certain boggy areas on the coasts of North and South Carolina. These plants get a lot of their nutrients from their insect diet, so they are able to live in areas with poor-quality soil. The Venus flytrap is not a tropical plant. It doesn't like extreme weather, but can tolerate mild winters.

? Many plants have amazing survival techniques. Find out about plants that have made amazing adaptations to ensure their survival.

Venus flytraps have special juices that prevent their catch from decaying before they've finished eating.

IF LOOKS COULD KILL . . .

Each trap looks like a small clamshell made up of two leaves that hinge together in the middle. The interior of each leaf is studded with short, super-sensitive hairs. The plant's dark red digestive glands are also inside these leaves. This vivid color helps to attract insects. The outer rim of each trap is lined with nectar that also helps draw in prey. Stiff, finger-like bristles line the edge of each trap. These mesh together when the trap closes to ensure no escape!

KISS OF DEATH

Since they're fairly small, Venus flytraps enjoy munching on spiders, flies, and other itty-bitty bugs. After forming an airtight seal around its catch, this plant starts to secrete digestive juices, much like those in your stomach. These plants consume the soft, inner parts of insects. But they can't digest the tough, outer parts called exoskeletons. Once the plant has finished eating and opens its trap, the exoskeleton is usually washed away by rain or wind. The digestive process can take from three to 12 days.

? It is illegal to pick Venus flytraps in the wild as they are endangered. What other plants are endangered? What are the reasons?

The Expert Says...

" Once a trap captures a bug, it requires about a week to digest it. Then it will reopen and be ready for a new bug. "

— Dr. Barry Rice, author of *Growing Carnivorous Plants*

Quick Fact

The time it takes for the Venus flytrap to reopen after closing around its prey depends on the size of the insect, the temperature, the age of the trap, and the number of times it has gone through this process.

EXOSKELETONS AND OTHER REMAINS

Some people grow Venus flytraps in their homes. Before you decide to buy one, you might want to read this interview with expert Dr. Barry Rice!

Q: What should I feed my Venus flytrap? Hamburger meat?

A: If you feed a Venus flytrap a bit of hamburger meat, it will probably die.

Venus flytraps expect bugs. Feed them anything else, and they will not like it. … If you want to feed your plants, you must find bugs. Bugs, bugs, bugs. I recommend caterpillars, flies, spiders, crickets, slugs … I do not recommend ants (the leaves are often damaged afterwards), moths (too much fuzz), butterflies (too cute), or beetles (too much sturdy exoskeleton). A warning about caterpillars … make sure that these or other bugs you feed to your plant cannot eat their way out! … I have been told that maggots make good food for Venus flytraps. … [But] maggots can usually escape from the traps, so … the maggot must first be "pierced with a toothpick."

Q: Can Venus flytraps digest human flesh?

A: … I figured this would be unlikely because surely the skin would be able to resist the puny enzymes from the plant. But here was a chance to prove it … I carefully selected four sizable chunks of skin (heh heh heh!) and … fed them to four different Venus flytraps … After a week, the traps opened. I had predicted the skin chunks would be relatively … unaffected … Was I ever wrong! The skin chunks were almost completely digested … So I guess that if you were to get caught by a sufficiently large Venus flytrap, your skin would easily be digested, and the plant would be able to proceed to your other internal tissues. Gross!

enzymes: *proteins involved in the process of digestion*

The inedible exoskeleton of this Venus flytrap's latest victim

Take Note

For such a little plant, the Venus flytrap has an amazing amount of stored power. Thank goodness their traps can only grow to a maximum of two inches. Otherwise, insects wouldn't be the only ones in trouble! Their deadly nature is evident in their snapping action. This plant gets a #7 ranking in our book.
• The Venus flytrap kills bugs but a swallowwort vine could kill a flytrap! Which one do you think is deadlier? Do you agree with our ranking? Explain.

5   4   3   2   1

6 MISTLETOE

Phoradendron *means "thief of the tree" in Greek. In this photo, green balls of mistletoe rob a host plant of food and water.*

TREE WITH MISTLETOE–SHUTTERSTOCK

SCIENTIFIC NAME: *Phoradendron serotinum* (fore-a-den-dron ser-oh-ty-num) (American mistletoe); *Viscum album* (vis-k-um al-buh-m) (European mistletoe); plus other species

NITTY-GRITTY: Mistletoe grows in clumps or as shrubs. Different species range in size from less than an inch to more than 32 ft. high! There are close to 2,000 species worldwide.

DEADLY DETAILS: Mistletoe is capable of living independently, but it prefers to rely on another tree's life support system.

Most of us know of mistletoe as the Christmas plant under which people are supposed to kiss in celebration. But, despite its romantic associations, mistletoe can be bad news for people and pets. It's safe to kiss under, but if the poisonous leaves or berries of the mistletoe are eaten, they can cause illness or death! We can avoid eating it, but trees are helpless when it comes to mistletoe's potential to harm. This evergreen is a tree's worst nightmare and it's found in forests all over the world. Just like the strangler fig, mistletoe settles high up in the branches of mature trees. It kills by stealing the host's food and water.

Believe it or not, mistletoe is actually an important link in maintaining biodiversity. Mistletoe provides food and shelter to many species of birds, small animals, and insects. Due to this fact, areas that have mistletoe have more diverse ecosystems. Mistletoe has also been valued for years for its medicinal qualities. It seems to have a lot going for it, but mistletoe still ranks at #6 on our list.

evergreen: *plant with green leaves throughout the entire year*
biodiversity: *measure of the variety and health of the life-forms in an ecosystem*

? What other plants play an important part in maintaining biodiversity?

23

MISTLETOE

HOME GROUND

Different species of mistletoe are found around the world, mostly in Africa, Asia, Australia, Europe, and in North and South America.

Mistletoe's super-sticky seeds are dropped onto unsuspecting trees by birds. Older, taller trees are the usual victims, as birds prefer to perch in their high branches. The seeds grab on and begin to grow out of the host's branches. Apple trees are mistletoe's favorite hosts. It also likes poplars, maples, ash, and willow trees.

IF LOOKS COULD KILL ...

All mistletoes are evergreens with waxy leaves and clusters of berries. Depending on the species, the berries can be white, purple, yellow, or other colors. European mistletoe has smooth-edged oval leaves that grow in pairs along its stems. This species has small clusters of two to six waxy, white berries. American mistletoe has shorter, broader leaves and longer clusters of 10 or more berries.

Quick Fact

Mistletoe has been used for centuries in home remedies. It is supposed to help lower blood pressure, relax tight muscles, and to stimulate the immune system. The same toxins that can harm in large amounts can be beneficial in small doses.

The Expert Says...

"Parasitism has an inherent sort of interest for a biologist, because parasites are clever plants or animals. They are very sophisticated in the way they make a living."

— Dr. Job Kuijt, Department of Biology, University of Victoria

inherent: *built-in characteristic*

Quick Fact

Pucker up! One legend says that Baldur, the Scandinavian god of peace, was killed with a mistletoe arrow. He was brought back to life and mistletoe became an emblem of love, not hate.

KISS OF DEATH

Mistletoe contains toxic chemicals that can seriously harm people and pets. If eaten, mistletoe causes upset stomachs, slowed heart rates, drowsiness, and sometimes even death.

Mistletoe has green leaves and is capable of photosynthesis, or turning sunlight into energy. Since it is a hemiparasite, or partial parasite, it uses this process for some of its energy. However, this lazy leech gets most of its nutrients and water through roots embedded in its host! Mistletoe plants get more nutrients from their host than they would on their own. They grow better when stealing from a host.

Once a tree gets stuck with one mistletoe shrub, it is likely to get more. As birds fly in to eat the berries of the first shrub, they drop more seeds on the host tree — and these seeds quickly sprout into more mistletoe plants! When too many parasitic mistletoe shrubs live off a tree, they usually end up killing it.

Timber companies don't like mistletoe because it weakens trees. It also lowers seed production in its host, which means fewer new trees in the future. Should these companies be allowed to kill mistletoe? Explain your answer.

Mistletoe's Many Guises

Most people can recognize mistletoe without any trouble. They've seen it deck the halls at Christmastime and know exactly what this partial parasite looks like. But, in a family of almost 2,000 species, this plant can be harder to identify than some people think. Read this descriptive list of some common mistletoe varieties.

Green Mistletoe

There are only two species of green mistletoe, which are both native to New Zealand. Green mistletoe flowers are small and green, of course! We think of mistletoe as having white berries, but it is not true of these two species. One of them has yellow berries and the other has purple fruit.

Scarlet Mistletoe

Thanks to its masses of bright red flowers, scarlet mistletoe is known for its looks. Amazingly, it's also known for its relatively harmless nature. It lives on other trees, but this species of mistletoe doesn't actually harm its host. This species is also known as beech mistletoe because of its habit of dwelling on various species of beech trees.

Dwarf Mistletoe

This obviously isn't the biggest of the bunch. But, despite its diminutive size, dwarf mistletoe is a major pain to the forest industry. Dwarf mistletoe preys on conifers, or cone-bearing trees native to North America. This species saps its host of nutrients and essential sugars. This makes the host weak and vulnerable to attacks from other predators. Dwarf mistletoe has no leaves, and grows clusters of branches that have been given the appropriately awful name of "witches' brooms"

Quick Fact

When the berries of dwarf mistletoe ripen, they explode. They shoot their seeds out to distances of up to 50 feet.

Take Note

Mistletoe ranks #6 on our list. A host tree doesn't stand a chance when infested with mistletoe. This plant can also be lethal to house pets and humans.
- Mistletoe kills its host, but it also attracts birds, insects, and animals into forest areas. Does mistletoe deserve to have a deadly reputation? Explain your answer.

The Latin name for common garden rhubarb is Rheum rhabarbarum. This translates roughly to "root of the barbarians."

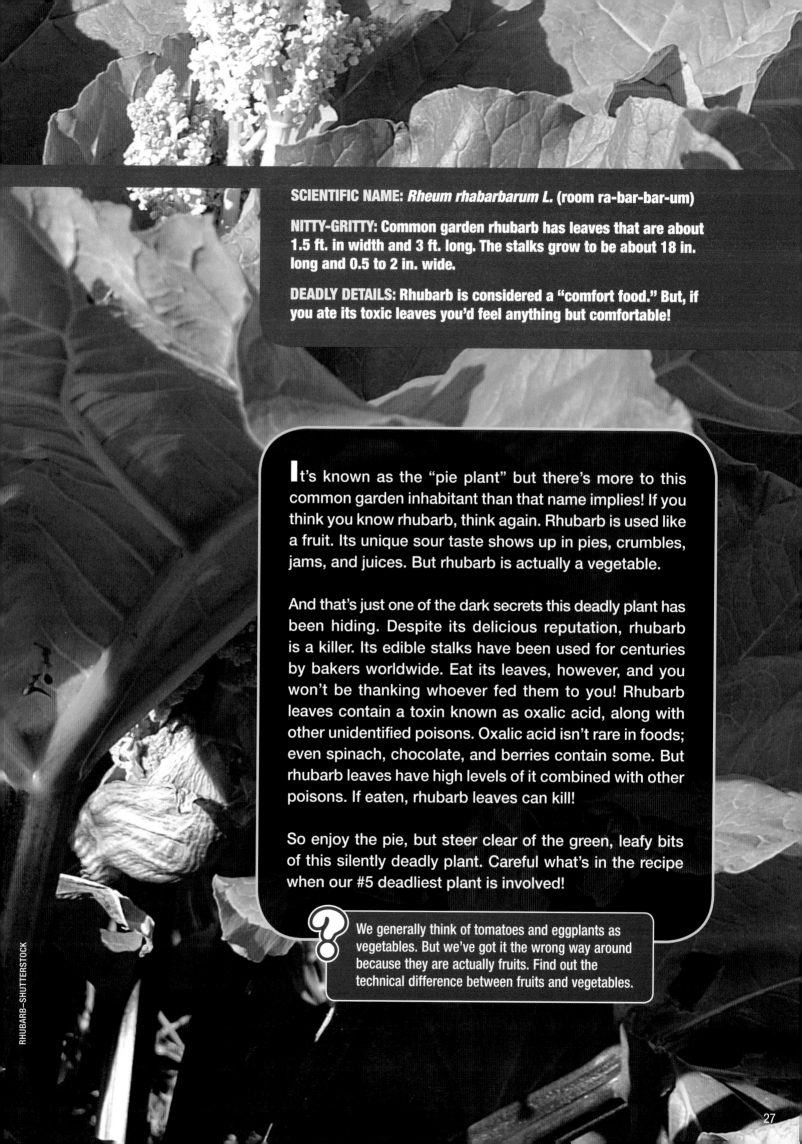

SCIENTIFIC NAME: *Rheum rhabarbarum L.* (room ra-bar-bar-um)

NITTY-GRITTY: Common garden rhubarb has leaves that are about 1.5 ft. in width and 3 ft. long. The stalks grow to be about 18 in. long and 0.5 to 2 in. wide.

DEADLY DETAILS: Rhubarb is considered a "comfort food." But, if you ate its toxic leaves you'd feel anything but comfortable!

It's known as the "pie plant" but there's more to this common garden inhabitant than that name implies! If you think you know rhubarb, think again. Rhubarb is used like a fruit. Its unique sour taste shows up in pies, crumbles, jams, and juices. But rhubarb is actually a vegetable.

And that's just one of the dark secrets this deadly plant has been hiding. Despite its delicious reputation, rhubarb is a killer. Its edible stalks have been used for centuries by bakers worldwide. Eat its leaves, however, and you won't be thanking whoever fed them to you! Rhubarb leaves contain a toxin known as oxalic acid, along with other unidentified poisons. Oxalic acid isn't rare in foods; even spinach, chocolate, and berries contain some. But rhubarb leaves have high levels of it combined with other poisons. If eaten, rhubarb leaves can kill!

So enjoy the pie, but steer clear of the green, leafy bits of this silently deadly plant. Careful what's in the recipe when our #5 deadliest plant is involved!

? We generally think of tomatoes and eggplants as vegetables. But we've got it the wrong way around because they are actually fruits. Find out the technical difference between fruits and vegetables.

RHUBARB

HOME GROUND

Various species of rhubarb are native to China, Russia, and India. These were initially cultivated for their medicinal qualities. It wasn't until the 16th century that new, edible species of rhubarb were grown in Britain and America. Rhubarb is a hardy plant, not needing much tender loving care. But it likes cold weather, moist surroundings, and lots of sun.

IF LOOKS COULD KILL . . .

Rhubarb is a tall plant with green, curly, heart-shaped leaves. Depending on the species, rhubarb stalks can range from deep red to light green and pale pink. Those curly leaves might seem tempting, but they're the ones people should avoid. During World War I people in Britain were encouraged to eat rhubarb leaves because they couldn't get other vegetables. Big mistake! Many people and animals were sickened, or even killed, by the poisonous foliage.

KISS OF DEATH

Though the whole plant contains oxalic acid, only rhubarb leaves have enough poison to cause harm. In general, a person would have to eat a huge serving of the leaves, about 11 pounds, for it to be fatal. But a lower dose can kill some people. Eating small quantities can make anybody sick. Symptoms of poisoning include weakness, trouble breathing, a burning mouth, stomach pain, and vomiting.

Quick Fact

You can harness this plant's deadly tendencies and use them to your advantage. Rhubarb leaves can be made into a pesticide against leaf-eating insects.

It's lucky that rhubarb stems aren't poisonous because they make delicious desserts, jams, and jellies!

The Expert Says...

" [Plants] have evolved to produce [poisonous substances] in order to deter animals from grazing on them and to keep insects from eating them. "

— Dr. Sharon M. Douglas, the Connecticut Agricultural Experiment Station

deter: *discourage*

Evil Edibles!

Rhubarb isn't the only plant with a split personality. Many foods that are perfectly safe to eat also contain poisons! Read this chart to find out which foods are hiding dark secrets.

The Good

Nutmeg

The spice we use to flavor desserts and other dishes is the seed of the *Myristica fragrans*, or nutmeg tree.

Potatoes

One of the world's biggest crops, potatoes are part of a perennial plant called *Solanum tuberosum*. Potatoes are part of the root of this plant.

Lima Beans

One of the world's healthiest foods, lima beans are part of the *Phaseolus lunatus* plant. They have fiber, protein, and other fantastic nutrients.

Apples

This fruit grows on *Malus domestica* or apple trees. They are part of the rose family. And don't worry, it's still true that an apple a day will help keep you healthy!

The Bad

You might like how it tastes on eggnog, but don't have too much! In large doses this spice causes "nutmeg poisoning," which can result in convulsions, dizziness, nausea, and even liver failure.

They can have white, orange, or purple flesh, but watch out when it's green! Potatoes contain glycoalkaloids, or poisons. When a potato turns green, it has been exposed to light and is more toxic. This poison can cause headaches, comas, and even death!

They provide great nutrition, but lima beans also contain cyanide. This poison causes stomach sickness, rapid breathing, and fainting. Luckily, boiling lima beans cuts the risk.

It's fine to enjoy apples raw or cooked, but careful with the seeds. Though it would take thousands of apple seeds to make a person sick, they shouldn't be eaten. Like lima beans, apple seeds contain cyanide. This poison keeps oxygen out of the blood and can cause death.

Quick Fact

When it was a popular medicine, dried rhubarb was pricey stuff! In the 16th and 17th centuries, it cost more than the popular spices that everyone longed to have.

Take Note

One has to know one's rhubarb before using it for pies or home remedies. Rhubarb is such a popular vegetable that people never thought its leaves could be poisonous. Many unsuspecting individuals have fallen victim to our #5 deadliest plant.

• Rhubarb root was originally used in Britain to treat stomach, colon, and liver illnesses. Today it is also used for medicinal purposes. Are you surprised that toxic plants can also be used to cure? Explain why or why not.

4 AZALEA

As little as 0.05 ounces of azalea nectar per pound of body weight can be toxic or lethal if ingested.

SCIENTIFIC NAME: Genus *Rhododendron* (rho-do-den-dron); Subgenus *Tsutsusi* (evergreen) and *Pentanthera* (deciduous)

NITTY-GRITTY: There are two main types of azaleas — the evergreen and the deciduous. Deciduous types lose their leaves in the fall. Some azaleas can grow to be over 13 ft. tall, while others spread along the ground.

DEADLY DETAILS: When eaten by people or animals, azaleas can cause abdominal and cardiovascular problems. All parts of the plants are toxic, as is honey made from the flowers.

Azaleas grow everywhere. Look anywhere in the world and you're likely to find azaleas. Nicknamed "royalty of the garden," they're prized by gardeners for their brightly-colored flowers. Despite their beautiful blooms, however, every part of the azalea plant is terribly toxic. Azaleas are so popular, we grow them inside our homes and outside in our gardens. Their proximity to people and to animals makes them deadlier than other plants on this list.

Through cultivation, people have been able to create many different species of azaleas. These species are created to withstand all sorts of different environments. Today, there is a type of azalea suitable for almost any territory. Even though there are thousands of azalea species, no one has been able to tame this beauty's poison!

cardiovascular: of, relating to, or affecting the heart and blood vessels
proximity: closeness

AZALEA

HOME GROUND

Azaleas grow naturally in North America, Asia, and parts of Eastern Europe. They like damp soil that is slightly acidic. Thanks to all the different varieties, there are azaleas that live in hot temperatures and others that thrive in the cold. Most types like shady areas under trees, but some can survive even in full sun.

IF LOOKS COULD KILL ...

They come in a wide range of colors — from fuchsia to purple, red to orange. Azalea flowers generally have five to seven petals and between five and 10 stamens. Both evergreen and deciduous azaleas shed their leaves in the fall. Evergreens, though, grow new leaves that stay on all winter. These are generally glossy and green, ranging from less than one inch to six inches in length. The fact that many azaleas have leaves throughout the winter adds to their deadly profile. These leaves look pretty tasty to animals starved for greens during the winter!

stamens: *parts of a flower that produce pollen*

KISS OF DEATH

Azaleas pack a pretty powerful punch! They contain cardiac glycosides. These chemicals are often used to make medicines for heart patients. When consumed directly from an azalea plant, though, these chemicals cause vomiting, salivation, abdominal pains, and tremors. Next the heart rate is affected and, if sufficient quantities are consumed, convulsions may occur. It's not over yet! If enough of the fatal foliage is eaten, the convulsions are followed by a loss of consciousness and eventual death.

Azaleas come in many colors

A bee collecting nectar from a yellow azalea!

The Expert Says...

" Poisonous plants are everywhere. More than 700 species of plants located in the United States and Canada have caused illness or death in humans. "

— Dawna L. Cyr, University of Maine

 List some common threats to plants, both here at home and around the world.

MAD HONEY'S HARMFUL HISTORY

People think of their sweethearts as being "as sweet as honey." These accounts reveal honey's not-so-sweet side. In fact, it's been a lethal weapon from ancient times to the present!

400s B.C. A Persian king, called Artaxerxes (ahr-tuh-zurk-seez) II, won a battle against Greece. After the victory, his army camped on nearby hills. These were covered with azaleas and other wildflowers. The triumphant soldiers ate lots of the area's honeycombs and wild honey. Soon, they were more miserable than merry! The hazardous honey made them feel disoriented, dizzy, and nauseous.

70s B.C. King Mithridates (mith-ri-da-teez) VI ruled an area in modern-day Turkey that borders the Black Sea. He spent many years defending his land against Pompey, a great Roman military leader. During one battle, Mithridates used mad honey as a weapon! He sneakily left jars of mad honey and honeycombs along the route taken by Pompey's army. Pompey's soldiers ate all the honey — and, sick to their stomachs and off balance, they were easily killed by Mithridates' soldiers!

A.D. 2002 The *Medical Research News* reported that a vacation to Turkey ended in a visit to the hospital for a group of tourists. The 19 tourists all ate honey and soon wished they hadn't! A few hours after they had eaten between 30 and 180 grams (1 and 8 tablespoons) of honey, they felt the substance's extreme effects! They vomited. They felt weak and had the chills. Their blood pressure and heart rates fell to dangerously low levels. Luckily, they received treatment in time and no one died.

Quick Fact

It's usually called "nectar of the gods", but when honey is made from azaleas, it's known as "mad honey"! When bees harvest nectar from azaleas, the resulting honey is as toxic as the plant.

Take Note

Azaleas take the #4 spot on our list. They are not only grown everywhere, but are highly desirable thanks to their bright colors and hardy nature. We put them where they don't grow naturally, bringing the danger even closer! Azaleas brighten the look of their environment. But they can be lethal to hungry animals in winter.

- A recent U.S. study found that 3.5% of all poisonings in the United States were caused by plants. How could you educate your classmates, friends, and family about the dangers of common plants?

This plant is also known as belladonna, which is Italian for beautiful lady. In the past, women used the juice from the berries as eye drops. These dilated their pupils, supposedly making their eyes more attractive. The drops also made their vision blurry and their hearts race!

TSHADE

SCIENTIFIC NAME: *Atropa belladonna* (a-troh-pah bel-uh-don-uh)

NITTY-GRITTY: This green leafy herb can grow to be over 3 ft. tall. There is also a creeping vine version. This plant is part of the *Solanaceae* (sole-ahn-ay-see-ee), or nightshade, family.

DEADLY DETAILS: Deadly nightshade is one of the most toxic plants found in the Western Hemisphere. The roots are the most poisonous parts. The leaves and dark berries aren't safe either and as few as three berries can poison a child.

This plant comes from a good family. But with a name like deadly nightshade, this species was pegged as a troublemaker from the start! The *Solanaceae* family consists of over 2,500 species. This family of plants is hugely diverse. Scientists are fascinated by the variety of plants in this botanical family. Because it is so lethal, the highly toxic deadly nightshade adds to the family's mystique. But it has another side. Atropine, the very thing that makes deadly nightshade poisonous, is used in small doses in medicines. It also has been used for centuries to do everything from dilating pupils to raising heart rates and opening up nasal passages.

Many common crops, like tomatoes, eggplants, and potatoes, as well as some garden plants are part of the *Solanaceae* family. But you're not scared of these common foods are you? No, it's deadly nightshade that you need to watch out for! This plant's wicked reputation marks it as deadly plant #3.

DEADLY NIGHTSHADE

HOME GROUND

Deadly nightshade is native to Europe, North Africa, and Asia. It now also grows wild in North America, after being introduced to the area from Europe years ago. Despite its aggressive personality, this plant is fussy when it comes to habitat. It thrives in shady areas and is sensitive to bright sunlight. Appropriately, deadly nightshade prefers to grow in gloomy, hidden places. It likes moist soil rich with limestone that's not too acidic. Deadly nightshade is not common as a garden plant and is usually considered a weed.

IF LOOKS COULD KILL . . .

Deadly nightshade hides its capacity to kill behind an unexciting, unalarming exterior. It looks like a typical small tree, complete with dull green leaves in the shape of a pointed oval. In the summer, the plants grow tiny purple flowers. Deadly nightshade's black, shiny berries are perhaps its most alluring feature.

KISS OF DEATH

Those berries might look good, but you won't like the effect they have on your body. People who try a taste of this berry can suffer from hallucinations, dry mouth, vision loss, rapid pulse and, in the worst cases, death. The entire plant is poisonous, and even touching the leaves can cause a rash. Animals are just as susceptible to the ill effects of deadly nightshade as people. Pets shouldn't be allowed to munch on this nasty weed.

susceptible: *likely to be affected*

Poisonous glossy, black berries on a deadly nightshade bush.

Quick Fact

Atropine, the poison found in deadly nightshade, can be used as an antidote against the effects of nerve gas. Atropine helps to block nerve gas from sticking to the nerves and damaging them.

The Expert Says...

"The truth is: some nightshades are good, others bad. You can fearfully avoid all, or learn who's who.

— Arthur Lee Jacobson, author and plant expert

All in the Family

This **FACT CHART** shows some familiar members of the huge *Solanaceae* botanical family.

TOBACCO

The most common species of this plant is *Nicotiana tabacum*. This plant is native to parts of South and Central America. Tobacco plants are used for their nicotine. Nicotine is an alkaloid and is poisonous. It is often used as an insect repellent.

alkaloid: *naturally occurring organic compound produced by plants*

EGGPLANT

The fruit of the *Solanum melongena* plant, eggplants are usually purple. But different species come in green, white, yellow, and mauve. Because of their repellent relatives, people once thought that eggplants were poisonous.

SWEET & HOT PEPPER

Make sure only edible varieties find their way into your kitchen! The ornamental varieties of the *Capsicum annuum* species are poisonous. On the plus side, edible varieties range from fiery Thai peppers to mild bell peppers.

TOMATO

Another plant that inherited a bad reputation is *Solanum lycopersicum*, or the common garden tomato. People used to think tomatoes were poisonous. And, they weren't far off! The fruit of the plant is safe. But, the leaves and stems contain the same poisons found in other members of the nightshade family.

? Nightshade has many edible cousins. Do you think this makes it more or less deadly? Explain.

Take Note

Deadly nightshade is not as common as its very familiar relatives. Its relatives don't kill, though. Many are actually a major food source worldwide. Substances extracted from deadly nightshade are used in medicines and antidotes. But when eaten, this plant is toxic even in very low doses and ranks at #3.
• Make a list of other plants in the book that have medicinal values in small doses. How do you think people first learned of these healing qualities?

2 OLEANDER

Oleander's poison is contained in its sap. But oleander leaves, flowers, branches, and bark remain poisonous even after the sap in them has dried.

SCIENTIFIC NAME: *Nerium oleander* (neer-ee-um oh-lee-an-der)

NITTY-GRITTY: Oleander can range in height from 6 to 20 ft. It is part of the *Apocynaceae* (ap-oh-sy-nay-see-ee), or dogbane family of plants.

DEADLY DETAILS: It looks like an average houseplant. But eating oleander leaves will make your heart beat at an abnormally rapid pace, or make it stop beating altogether!

You might not think such a harmless looking plant could make it to second place on a list of deadliest plants. But like azaleas, oleander is a demon in disguise. With its beautiful flowers and intoxicating scent, the deadly oleander plant has managed to make people forget about its true nature. This killer is very hardy — it can survive with very little water and doesn't mind the heat. It is so popular that it is found all over the world in homes, offices, shopping malls, gardens, and along roadsides.

But beware! What you don't know about oleander could kill you. Oleander's poison is contained in its sap. But oleander leaves, flowers, branches, and bark remain poisonous even after the sap in them has dried. It's not just dangerous when eaten. Drinking oleander extract, eating honey made from oleander flowers, even inhaling fumes from burning oleander wood can cause serious symptoms and even death.

 We mark toxic household chemicals with warning labels and put childproof caps on medicines. But we allow lethal household plants to be sold without warning signs. Are they any less dangerous than household poisons? Explain your answer.

OLEANDER

HOME GROUND

This species is native to the Mediterranean, Asia, Portugal, and Morocco, but is now found around the world. Oleander is a tropical plant that prefers warm temperatures, direct sunlight, and a moist environment. It generally grows outdoors in warmer regions and indoors, as a houseplant, in colder regions.

IF LOOKS COULD KILL ...

Oleander is an evergreen shrub with thick and leathery, dark green leaves. The leaves are generally from four to seven inches long. People often trim the lower branches of oleanders to make them look like small trees. The oleander's showy flowers are its best feature. They are approximately two inches in diameter and have five petals. Before people created different oleander species, oleander blooms were usually white or pink. Today, thanks to cross-pollination, breeders have been able to grow oleanders with flowers in a wide range of colors from lilac and salmon to pale yellow and scarlet. These flowers often have a sweet, alluring scent.

cross-pollination: *transfer of pollen from the flower of one plant to a different type of plant*

KISS OF DEATH

Oleander's deadly poison is mostly found in its sticky, milky sap. This sap contains cardiac glycosides, chemicals that cause the heart to beat stronger and faster. Apart from setting victims' hearts into overdrive, these chemicals also cause severe stomach problems, dizziness, low blood pressure, and blurred vision. Getting any of this poisonous sap into your system causes bodily harm and possibly death. A single leaf can cause a dangerous reaction. Ingesting more than this has killed pets, farm animals, and humans.

? Why do you think plant poisons are usually bitter? How might this be beneficial to both humans and plants?

Quick Fact

Oleander sap tastes extremely bitter — like rotten lemon. Thankfully, most people can't stand the taste of it! But for those with strong stomachs or no sense of taste a dose of the poison can be fatal.

The Expert Says...

"[We cannot] allow their loveliness to lure us into forgetting their toxicity ... There have been ... poisonings resulting from using oleander branches as skewers to roast hot dogs and from children sucking nectar from the flowers."

— Courtney Denney, University of California Master Gardener

Oleander growing on a Mediterranean beach

10   **9**   **8**   **7**   **6**

WILL THE REAL HAZARD PLEASE STAND UP?

Toxic plants are not something to be taken lightly. But remember, as dangerous as they may be, you don't have to live in fear of foliage. Here are some poisons by the numbers, taken from the American Association of Poison Control Centers' 2005 Annual Report.

2,031,538 Total number of unintentional poisonings in humans

131,336 Total number of animals reported to have been poisoned

68,847 Total number of people who reported plant poisonings

22,531 Number of people who reported fluoride toothpaste poisoning

17,730 Total reported pen ink poisonings in humans

4,639 People poisoned by drinking liquid dishwasher detergent

766 Number of reported oleander poisonings in humans

Quick Fact

Heavily **diluted** oleander extracts have been used in medications to treat everything from muscle cramps and asthma to cancer and skin irritations. But don't forget that it has also been used to poison rats.

diluted: *watered down*

Some other plants in this book have the same "kill or cure" powers as oleander. Find out what they are and research other such plants.

Take Note

Oleander made it to #2 because it is deadly to both animals and humans, even in very small doses. Not only can a single leaf kill, but it's also lurking right under our noses as nothing more than a pretty plant or shrub.
- What do you think? Is oleander dangerous enough to be banned?

Long ago, poison hemlock was used in medicines. The only problem? It was hard for doctors to tell how much would cure and how much would kill!

LOCK

SCIENTIFIC NAME: *Conium maculatum* (ko-nee-um mak-yoo-lay-tum)

NITTY-GRITTY: Poison hemlock is a deadly distant cousin of carrots, caraway, and parsley. It is a green leafy plant that can grow up to 10 ft. tall.

DEADLY DETAILS: This plant hides its toxic nature, and tricks humans and animals into tasting its deadly poison.

? Have you ever thought about what it would be like to live off the land? Make a list of safe edible plants found in your part of the world.

How long could you live, with nothing but your instincts and the wild foods you found to keep you going? Before you get too confident, you might want to brush up on your knowledge of edible plants. There are killer plants out there masquerading as harmless ones! Poison hemlock's leaves look like parsley and its roots look like parsnips, but you wouldn't want poison hemlock on your plate. Its clever disguise makes it all the more deadly. Poison hemlock easily attracts unsuspecting victims and gets them with its fast-acting toxins. It doesn't matter which parts you eat either; they're all deadly. So watch out!

Avoid a case of mistaken identity and learn more about our deadliest plant.

POISON HEMLOCK

Close-up of poison hemlock seeds

Close-up of poison hemlock flowers

HOME GROUND

Poison hemlock is native to Europe and South Africa. But today, poison hemlock thrives around the world, especially in Asia, Australia, and North and South America. Poison hemlock likes very moist soils. It grows near streams, ditches, and other surface waters. It is a very common weed and can be found in many urbanized areas.

IF LOOKS COULD KILL ...

Poison hemlock, along with its lethal relative water hemlock, can cause illness or death in animals and people. An ace at disguise, this lethal plant resembles wild carrot (also known as Queen Anne's lace), parsley, fennel, and parsnip.

A good way to identify poison hemlock is to look for its stem, which is smooth and hollow and covered with reddish purple spots. Poison hemlock also has delicate, triangular leaves that can be up to 20 inches long. From June to July, these plants sprout clusters of tiny, white, lacy flowers. The roots of poison hemlock look like wild parsnips. They're so alike that many people have eaten the white, fleshy, toxic roots by mistake and paid a high price!

KISS OF DEATH

All parts of poison hemlock plants are toxic. The roots, stems, flowers, leaves, and seeds all contain potent toxic alkaloids. The seeds contain the highest concentration of poison. The poison is so lethal it can even cause toxic reactions when inhaled. Even if it doesn't kill you, poison hemlock can cause unsightly symptoms like dilated pupils, convulsions, headaches, dizziness, and a weak, rapid pulse.

Quick Fact

Water hemlock is even more toxic than poison hemlock. It kills so quickly that there usually isn't even time to seek help! But, since it prefers marshes and wetlands, it's not as much of a threat as the more common poison hemlock.

The Expert Says...

" The problem is with city people who ... don't know the difference between poisonous and safe plants. They might end up having poison hemlock right in their backyard. "

— Joe Boggs, Ohio State University horticulture specialist

Study these leaves, your life could depend on it! Water hemlock (left) and poison hemlock (right)

Poison Hemlock 101

Dr. Steven Dewey is an Extension Weed Specialist and Professor of Plant Science at Utah State University. In this e-mail he teaches us about poison hemlock's grisly grip.

From: Christine
To: Steven Dewey
Subject: Poison Hemlock Question

Dear Dr. Dewey,

Could you please tell me a little bit about poison hemlock? How deadly is it and where is it found? How can people avoid the plant's lethal toxins?

From: Steven Dewey
To: Christine
Re: Poison Hemlock Question

Hi Christine,

Poison hemlock is deadly. It is the plant reported to have killed Socrates. I also know that it looks very much like wild carrot. It would be easy to make a fatal mistake if someone experimenting with wild edible plants were to confuse the two. All parts of the plant are poisonous, both fresh and dried. The stems of poison hemlock are hollow. They might be considered by a curious and resourceful youth as a potential blow-gun or drinking straw. I'm pretty sure that putting a stem (green or dried) in the mouth would result in enough toxin exposure to cause illness or worse.

Poison hemlock is primarily a weed of waste places. The plant has a very disagreeable odor, and animals will normally avoid eating it. The exception is when dried hemlock is intermixed with hay. If hay is harvested before removing poison hemlock from fields, it could result in the poisoning of livestock. I've heard it said that dairy cows fed contaminated hay could pass on some of the toxin through their milk (if the amount they consumed was insufficient to actually kill the cow).

The best way to avoid the toxin is to learn to recognize and then avoid touching the plant. To teach my university students to identify hemlock I require that they collect and preserve a specimen. I insist that they wash their hands soon after handling any amount of hemlock.

— Steve

disagreeable: *unpleasant, offensive*

? Are there plants other than hemlock that cause this much trouble if they are mistaken for something else? Make a list of other disguised killers.

Take Note

Poison hemlock does such a good job of pretending to be something it's not that it ranks #1. This killer pretends to be edible; the worst disguise of all! It is easy to find and people are interested in eating it because it looks familiar to them.

• Poison hemlock is only native to Europe and South Africa. Why would people import a poisonous plant into their countries?

5   4   3   2   1

We Thought …

Here are the criteria we used in ranking the 10 deadliest plants.

The deadly plant:
• Makes its victims extremely sick
• Kills its victims
• Has fast-acting toxins
• Is found all over the world
• Is common in populated areas
• Is often confused for another, harmless plant
• Is harmful to other plants
• Is harmful to animals
• Is harmful to humans

What Do You Think?

1. Do you agree with our ranking? If you don't, try ranking these plants yourself. Justify your ranking with data from your own research and reasoning. You may refer to our criteria, or you may want to draw up your own list of criteria.

2. Here are three other deadly plants that we considered but in the end did not include in our top 10 list: castor bean, rhododendron, and poinsettia.
   • Find out more about them. Do you think they should have made our list? Give reasons for your response.
   • Are there other deadly plants that you think should have made our list? Explain your choices.

Index